So You Want to Learn Spanish?

KEITH WALTERS

ISBN-13: 978-0985663704

ISBN-10: 0985663707

This book is available at special quantity discounts to use as premiums and sales promotions, or for use in corporate or educational training programs. For more information, please logon to http://tbdpub.wix.com/tbdp or write to True Blue Dolphin Publishing, 3024 W. Michigan Ave., Phoenix, AZ, 85053.

Cover design by Joe Cordaro

DEDICATION

To my readers, I whole-heartedly appreciate your time, excitement and determination to learn Spanish. This language is my passion too. I hope that my excitement will help keep you engaged to move forward. May you find valuable and insightful tips and resources within these pages. I am excited for you. Your journey is just beginning!

CONTENTS

ACKNOWLEDGMENTS

I am grateful to Joe McShane, my loving husband, who has encouraged and helped me write this book. Through his willingness to make copies for editing to giving me the space and time I needed to concentrate and write, I owe him this debt of gratitude for sticking by and picking up the slack where necessary. *Mil gracias* to Connie García, one of my former high school Spanish teachers, who graciously reviewed and edited this book as well as took time out of her busy schedule to write the foreword. I would like to thank my editor, Jill, who left acknowledging her contribution to this book completely up to me. Without her passion and commitment reviewing and going over the same sections forwards and backwards, this book would not have the linguistic spark it does. Finally, to my family, friends, and co-workers who have cheered me on and helped me stay motivated to complete this book. Thank you all from the bottom of my heart!

KEITH WALTERS

FOREWORD

There is an old Spanish proverb that says this: *El que sabe dos lenguas vale por dos*. Translated, it means, "He who knows two languages is worth two (people)". When looking at the United States of America as a diverse country (more than ever before), we can easily see the value of knowing two languages, especially Spanish. However, it is easy to think (and many do) that everyone should just speak English. Why is that? As a young person, I was blessed to be able to study abroad and go to college in both Spain and Mexico. I witnessed firsthand the abilities of many people from around the world that spoke three or more languages. And yet, as a nation, we often "fight" against knowing two or more languages, so much so, that many states continually try to create laws to keep everything "English Only". As a foreign language teacher, it makes no sense to me! Knowing another language challenges the "norm". It increases brain function, improves the knowledge of the L1 (first language), and breaks down stereotypes and communication barriers. While traveling around Europe, I heard this joke all the time: What do you call a person who speaks three languages? –Trilingual. What do you call a person who speaks two languages? –Bilingual. What do you call a person who speaks only ONE language? –American. How sad!

From an educational standpoint, it is important to see that more and more, schools across the nation need to have knowledge of Spanish in order to be able to communicate with students and their families. Students are attending our schools with all levels of English (from NO English to some English) and teachers are faced with the difficult (but not impossible) task of differentiating lessons in order to meet the needs of their students and so the students will pass the high-stakes, standardized tests. The idea of "sink or swim" (putting students in all English-only classes with no support) may not be in the best interest of our students. So, some knowledge of Spanish can be helpful and can help to build relationships with parents and students. Also, it should be stated that ANY students who are school-aged (here legally or illegally) MUST be given services in education while on U.S. soil – it's the law!

In our communities, knowledge of Spanish can also help to bridge gaps between businesses and clients. When there are bilingual staff members/employees, Spanish-speaking clients may feel more comfortable and may be more inclined to return to that business for services. There are a couple of "perks" for knowing a second language when thinking about careers/jobs: 1) Knowing a second language can sometimes help an applicant to be hired over those that only speak English and 2) A higher wage, offered with some jobs, may also be a benefit.

For a person who seeks to travel the world, knowing another language can only be something positive! The chances of being taken advantage of as a tourist, being put in harm's way, being ripped off, etc. lessen with the knowledge of a foreign language. The world opens up to you. Language and culture are intertwined and cannot be split apart. When you learn a language, you learn about the culture of the people who speak that language and the barriers between people seem to disappear! It allows you to really understand the saying, "When in Rome, do as the Romans do".

The ideas above are ones that I have shared over the years in my Spanish classes with many students. Keith Walters, the author of this book, *So You Want to Learn Spanish?*, was one such student so many years ago. I feel honored to write the foreword for his book. He is correct in saying that learning a second language takes TIME and practice and if you want to learn Spanish well, you just have to keep trying. To add to this guide for people wanting to learn Spanish, I would like to share one last idea. As a student living abroad in Spain, I had the unique experience of using an *intercambio* (which literally means "mutual exchange"). I found a person on our local university campus who advertised on the student bulletin board that he wanted to improve his English skills. Because I wanted to work on my Spanish skills, I gave him a call. We would meet once a week for two hours, for almost the whole semester at different coffee shops. We set up a specific time and place and for one hour, we only spoke in Spanish and the next hour, we only spoke in English. We each brought to the session whatever it was we were wanting to work on: vocabulary, grammar, homework assignments from our university classes, song lyrics to translate, poetry, etc. It was the best of both worlds. And I learned so much more than a textbook could ever teach me because we were both getting a native speaker's perspective, and enjoying a new friendship over a *café con leche* (coffee with milk) once a week. So, my advice, is take Keith's advice, use the book as a guide to learn Spanish and enjoy the journey!

Connie García
Spanish/English as a Second Language Teacher
Master of Arts in At-Risk Education and Master of Arts in
Social & Multicultural Foundations in Education

CHAPTER 1: INTRODUCTIONS

Growing up, I knew I loved Spanish. My older brother studied Spanish in high school and in college, and growing up, I wanted to do what he did. My passion for Spanish ignited, sparked by my brother's interest. My brother, however, didn't have an easy time with it -- he actually struggled with learning the language. I would find him studying the language for many hours at a time at the kitchen table. His textbook lay opened while he would wrote down answers to questions for the lesson (*lección*). He would teach me little sentences like "What time is it?" (*¿Qué hora es?*) or "My name is Keith" (*Me llamo* Keith). Probably because he spent so much time studying, and engaging me through his learning, Spanish was just another extension of my connection to him. Though I did not learn very much other than some simple words and sentences, it was enough to whet my appetite for this passionate language.

In my hometown, the local public school system allowed students to begin their study of a foreign language in junior high school. Due to some sort of glitch at school which didn't become apparent until after I began seventh grade, I was never enrolled in Spanish class until a whole year later -- eighth grade. The rest of my grade was an entire year ahead of me at that point. I felt awful and I knew I was at a big disadvantage compared to my classmates. And I knew that I'd have to overcome this challenge on my own.

I studied hard and found ways to speak Spanish to my mother, my friends, and even my dog. I even spoke out loud to myself. Yes, talking to yourself can be quite beneficial and fun when you are inspired to learn a language. You get practice — and there's no one who'll criticize you! There was a passion inside me to soak up every bit of Spanish I could — the language, the culture, the people and the history. I often dreamed of visiting the various places I was learning about in my textbooks and from my teachers.

Passion was something that helped drive me to succeed in Spanish. It is an ingredient that will help anyone learning any language (or anything else!). Not many people find languages fun, which is a shame, because it can be tremendous fun. If you don't include yourself in the group of people who are already passionate about learning Spanish, you can use another of your passions to help. Take a moment to identify what gets you excited. Whether it's the outdoors, electronics, literature, writing, watching movies or television, identify your passion, and then find a way to connect it with the language you want to learn. By mixing the two together, you will not only find enjoyment in something that you're already enthusiastic about, but it will also engage the parts of your brain that will help you excel in your language learning.

My passion drove me to major in Spanish in college. As part of that, I went on a couple of college trips, first to the Yucatán Peninsula in Mexico, and then later on, I studied in Antigua, Guatemala for a couple of months. I took the equivalent of the Foreign Service exam for native Guatemalans, which was a requirement for my study abroad experience, and I passed the written and oral parts with near-native ability in Spanish. Outside of school, I used my bilingual skills to help tutor, teach, interpret and translate. I helped high school students study and learn the language. I tutored a "soon-to-be" mother who was adopting a little boy from Honduras, and assisted her as an interpreter when she needed help communicating with the adoption agency. I translated texts for church services from Spanish into English for my pastor. There were many ways for to test out various jobs that used Spanish. It was a great method to see where my strengths and weaknesses were.

I dabbled a bit in these various areas, though I knew my heart was not really in being an interpreter. But I discovered a real love for translating the written word. There was something about how a writer using Spanish stirred up my passion for the language. I would find stories, news articles, web sites, even advertisements in Spanish and try my hand at translating them into English. From time to time I would try the reverse. It was sort of a game I played to challenge myself. Ultimately, I was absolutely certain that one thing I wanted to do in my life was help others gain new perspectives that can only come from learning a language other than English.

Since graduating college, I have taught Spanish in group settings as well as one-on-one situations. Interpreting and translating have given way a bit while I pursue other new interests, but I still stay in the game through various online translation groups that I've subscribed to for years. All of my experiences, trials and tribulations have helped me become a better language learner.

From my long experience, I'm happy to bring you these tips and recommendations to help you with learning Spanish. As with everything in life, there is no guarantee that you will actually learn the language. But there's a good chance, because you are in charge of that destiny, and you are already taking action.

The Spanish Language and People

A huge part of the population of this planet speaks Spanish. To a great extent, that's because Spain once reigned over an empire where the sun never set. Its territories not only reached North, Central and South America, but it touched as far East as the Philippines. The mother country of the Spanish language is located on Europe's Iberian Peninsula. Portugal shares the

3

peninsula on the southwestern side, which is interesting because even though they're neighbors in a somewhat isolated situation – they don't speak Spanish there.

Many cities within the United States have large Spanish-speaking populations, such as New York, Chicago, Phoenix and Los Angeles. Spanish is spoken in various parts of the South and Southwest by people who may be descendants of Native American and Spanish colonial settlers. Many Spanish-speaking immigrants have crossed the U.S. southern border, risking life and limb to make a better life for themselves and their families. The Americas, which include North America, Central America, and South America, contain millions of very poor and humble people who work very hard for their families. Some live in rural areas that even maintain their own indigenous traditions.

I think it is important to understand some statistical information on this population – at least as it impacts the United States. The United States Census for 2010 released data on Hispanic populations and Spanish-speaking peoples. The data still supports that Hispanics are the largest minority population in the United States. In the May, 2011 issue of the *2010 Census Briefs* on "The Hispanic Population: 2010", it mentions that 1 in every 4 counties had an increase in Hispanics of over twice their size since 2000. That's a huge population increase. According to the *2008 American Community Survey*, 35 million U.S. residents who are 5 years and older speak Spanish in the home. Granted more than half said they spoke English "very well", but that still leaves a large portion with minimal or no English-speaking abilities. It also goes to show you that despite their ability to speak English, they still use Spanish within the home.

Throughout all travels, Latino people have been the most kind, caring and compassionate people I have ever known. I have not encountered a single person who judged or held things against anyone. That aspect is one that I find refreshing and I wish that we in the U.S. could emulate it more. That's not to say there probably aren't some unkind people there somewhere, because every land has its pluses and minuses. The

Latino cultures are rich with their own culture, which is manifested in many ways, including their music, dance and food. In a sense, the Latino cultures are a true melting pot of African, European and indigenous peoples. They have accepted other cultures into their own. Perhaps it is this quality that will keep the Spanish language thriving for centuries to come.

The Purpose of this Book

This book exists to help you find ways to learn and improve your Spanish. In time, you will become more confident in your reading, writing, listening and speaking skills. Practice is the key to your success with Spanish. There is truth to that sage wisdom. Each time you utter a word, a phrase or a sentence in Spanish, you will stick your neck out there for the entire world to see – and hear. You will make blunders and you may make some ghastly mistakes. You will sound like a gringo, a foreigner, because you are one. I am giving you permission to make mistakes and feel all of the associated feelings and to accept them as necessary truths in your journey to learning another language. And know that as long as you give it your all, you will prevail.

This book is unique. I wrote it because I couldn't find one like it anywhere. What makes this book special is that it will help you right away to develop strategies to learn, maintain, and improve your Spanish abilities. Whether you are starting from square one or know some Spanish already, you will get some ideas about how to improve your language skills through this book.

I wish that I had this book when I was just starting to learn the language. It would have helped me avoid a lot of unhelpful gimmicks and wasted money along the way. Many Spanish teachers might give you some of this information, but none of them would be able to give you all of my recommendations and techniques. Use this book to guide you through your journey in learning Spanish.

One thing to always remember is that your knowledge will grow over time. For some people, each step forward may also take them back a few steps. They will ebb and flow with each passing day. Their energy may be fine one day helping them make leaps and bounds, and then the next day, they may barely have the energy to do their regular daily activities. That's okay. This is your journey, an adventure, something exciting you are embarking on. Take it with a grain of salt and a smile. You can learn Spanish, and you can learn it at your own pace. You can do anything you set your mind to doing. The main point I am trying to get across is to set realistic goals, then get out there and do it. You realistically may not be a fluent Spanish-speaker after just a short number of months. But if you are true to yourself, your capabilities, your determination, and your follow-through, you will reach your Spanish fluency goals. After all, Roman was not built in just one day. The same can be stated for any foreign language you learn.

How to Use this Book

There are many ways for you to practice and learn Spanish in this book, which is full of tips and tricks to use to help you feel more confident and secure while learning the language. You don't have to do everything in this book, nor will you be able to do everything. But do what you can. Some of the suggestions in this book may seem strange, but go with it and give it a try – you won't get hurt! And the thing you thought was strange may just turn out to provide the motivation you need to help you succeed.

There are three parts to this book. The first part discusses active and passive non-techie ways to learn Spanish. Part two complements that by covering all the technological methods available to you. Part three delves into identifying the learner you are and giving you some solid learning recommendations and resources. I recommend reading through the entire book making note of methods and techniques that you want to try. You might not get to all of them the first time around, but come back to this book and give other suggestions a chance. Set up a step-by-step plan to make it happen.

There's some useful information about learning in chapter 16, which explores various types of learners, and how you can determine which learning type you are. This might arm you with sufficient knowledge to hone in on the various techniques in the other chapters. So even though it's at the end of the book, think about taking a look at this chapter early on. The important thing is to have fun exploring different ways you can learn Spanish. It is my hope that you gain more knowledge and wisdom to help you achieve everything you want from Spanish, and from life.

Some techniques will require that you have a computer and access to the Internet. Other suggestions will seem expensive. As I stated before, you don't have to adopt them all. If money is an issue, there are low-cost ways to learn and maintain your foreign language. Pick and choose what you can afford and want to do – every little bit will help in some way. The important thing is that you relax and have fun.

Learning Spanish is fantastic! You get to express all the things you want to say by using a code -- a linguistic code. One summer in college when I worked as a cashier for a regional department store, a couple of Spanish-speaking customers came to my register to check out. I conducted my end of the transaction in English as that is the language they used with me, while they continued to speak Spanish to each other. When our employee-customer transaction finished, I threw out something similar to an enthusiastic *¡Gracias por las compras; regresen pronto!* (Thank you for shopping; come again!) in Spanish. Their eyes widened and they smiled back. It was such great fun to surprise people that with my knowledge of Spanish (and perhaps the fact that I knew what they were saying in Spanish).

There are so many wonderful ways to use your Spanish skills. I helped an elderly lady at my church with information and announcements. She was from Central America and spoke very little English. To see her face light up each time we talked in Spanish brought sheer joy to my heart. Certainly, with

Latinos as the largest minority in the U.S., there is a time and place to prepare you for that new world where "minorities" will become the "majority." A world where Spanish will be uncommon. Your neighbors, friends, co-workers and fellow community members will be speaking Spanish. Now is your time to embark on that journey, and enjoy learning Spanish!

PART 1: FUN RETRO LEARNING!

CHAPTER 2: CLASSES

There are all types of Spanish classes, ranging from typical high school or college level classes, all the way up to classes at dedicated language schools, and even online classes. This discussion will be about high school and college classes, language schools, conversational classes you can find in various places in your community, and classes specifically dedicated to senior citizens.

Usually when a person goes about learning something, they think of taking a class in it. When it comes to learning Spanish, it's no different. In fact, classes are the most common way of learning a language, and they are an excellent way to learn Spanish. Your teacher can guide you through, little by little. Of course, your teacher should be skilled and proficient in Spanish, be able to challenge you to learn, and should also have the compassion and patience to let you make mistakes. However, taking classes is also one of the most expensive ways to learn a language, and there are other drawbacks you should be aware of, too.

Learning a language in a group can be lots of fun. For one thing, classes are wonderful environments for motivation. If you witness others engaged in the learning, you will more likely than not want to follow the crowd and try hard to be interested as well. Clever teachers use psychological methods to maximize peer pressure in a positive way to keep students focused and actively learning.

Instructors provide some very practical and useful tips that they have found to work well. One such professor gave me a tip about how to practice my double "rr" sound, which is common in Spanish, and sounds much like a rolling or trilled "r." What helps is realizing where your tongue is positioned in your mouth as you repeat the word "ladder." Saying it faster and faster will help simulate the experience you would get of pronouncing the double "rr" sound. As you improve, you can incorporate that sound in real Spanish words.

The most incredible aspect of classroom learning is that you have a self-contained laboratory in which to practice speaking Spanish to others as much as you possibly can. You can really screw up the language in this environment, and no one will make fun of you. Don't worry, no one expects you to speak perfect Spanish here. It's a safe zone for learning. Your teacher is there to help facilitate and make you feel comfortable learning this beautiful language. Indeed, your Spanish instructors make all this possible for everyone in class. The Spanish teachers I have known are some of the most dedicated and passionate educators I have ever witnessed. I applaud all of them for their efforts to make language learning fun, interactive, memorable and meaningful.

Of course, not everything can be sunshine and rainbows. The disadvantage to classroom learning is that each person is learning the language at a different pace from the next person. A teacher must try to keep the class moving at a consistent pace so that faster learners will not get bored and slower learners will be challenged enough – but in reality, that is extremely difficult to do, even for great teachers. Seeking a "happy medium," teachers often try to teach to the "average" student in the group. This is not always appropriate -- especially if you happen to be the student who is not average, but rather you are on either spectrum of the learning scale. Unfortunately, given limited resources (time and money) and the size of classrooms in general, there is not a lot that can be done about that, as much as the education system tries. It's been this way for eons.

Another caveat to consider is the amount of Spanish that you are learning. Classes are designed so that a specific amount of knowledge and material are covered in the allotted time. If you run out of time or material, that is just too bad, that is so sad. Of course, some teachers may move forward a bit, but not too much, as that would throw off future classes. So time is definitely a limiting factor.

Practice time in classes is limited by the number of people in the class. The teacher only has so much time for the class – there's a specific start time, and a non-negotiable end time. (The dismissal bell may even ring!) When divided up, a small portion of class time is devoted to having the students actually speak Spanish.

But perhaps you can find some classes specifically for conversational Spanish, which are all the craze right now. They are designed to focus less on grammar and parts of speech, and more on stepping up and going for it, and embracing the actual speaking of the language. Again, these classes are limited by the number of students in the class. Most activities will be group activities where you will have to share the amount of time speaking the language with other students. There will be some activities where you will need to read aloud or present some information to the class. They will focus on you learning the grammar and vocabulary information outside of class, so you can spend more time speaking and practicing in class. And unfortunately, you will always have some students who do not prepare at all mixed in with the others who do all the necessary and prescribed preparation. So it will be a mixed bag in any given class.

Many seniors love to take continuing education courses at local community colleges or community centers. These can be wonderful classes where teachers and students devote time and care to a passion of language learning. Classes dedicated to this group may evolve around travel. Some seniors typically have more disposable income, more time, and make plans to visit other countries. Latin American countries and Europe (including Spain) are among the most popular trips for globe-trotting seniors. A good conversation class will help them develop the confidence and skills they will need for such excursions. There won't be a lot of grammar drills or vocabulary lists to memorize here. Instead, the focus is on real-life situations that might come up, and how best to understand, express and handle them appropriately in Spanish. Various cultural aspects are brought up and include travel tips, such as cultural practices you can participate in, and those to avoid. These classes will help get you by while you're in a Spanish-speaking country, but they lack sufficient emphasis on the language structure for you to be able to create and navigate the language in depth, and without relying on stock phrases.

Please don't get me wrong: I do advocate for people to take Spanish classes, which is how I learned the language, myself. I also believe they provide wonderful insights and support when learning a language. I'm just trying to present you with the whole picture of what to expect using this method of language learning.

Language schools are fantastic. If you're lucky you'll be able to find a school that pairs you up, one on one, with a native Spanish-speaker. I attended one such school when I lived in Guatemala, where students had specific attention from the teacher and multiple opportunities to speak the language, and the freedom to make mistakes without being made to feel uncomfortable. If the language school is in another country, you often have many opportunities to travel with your teacher and see the sights, and learn more about the country and its people. I would recommend attending a language school if you have the funds to do so.

Of course, there are downsides to everything and language schools are no exception. People attend language schools for short periods of time, one to four weeks, or maybe more depending upon your available time and funds. Students experience firsthand the rich culture and language of the people whose language they're studying, but unless you are Mr. or Ms. Moneybags, this is not practical for a majority of people. Many adults have other obligations (such as putting food on the table and taking care of their families). One can't simply drop everything to spend a month or two in a foreign country to learn a language. But if this is no problem for you, then consider the money needed to cover tuition at the school and living expenses (room and board, meals, insurance, etc.). A student is usually not permitted to work while attending a language school unless you obtain a worker visa for a specific period of time. Your day consists of attending class, going on excursions, interacting with a group and/or your teacher, spending evenings preparing for the next day, and perhaps even enjoying a night out on the town.

Some U.S. private schools, universities both public and private as well as some organizations and companies have developed immersion classes or programs where students spend their entire school day speaking, reading, and writing in the target language (in this case, Spanish) – and no English is allowed! Students learn all of their subjects – math, science, history, literature, and so on, in Spanish. These are usually cheaper options than traveling to another country and spending lots of money on room and board. If you want to save on dough, then I would recommend attending an immersion school or class as the next best thing to provide you with more opportunities to speak the language.

The important things to note when selecting a class are opportunities. Will you have ample opportunity to speak, to write, to read, and to learn the grammar and fine points of the language, enough to be able to speak, read, and write on your own? In the beginning, there is a lot to learn and a class setting, which is often a familiar situation for many people, is a great way to learn Spanish. The teacher and your classmates can help hold you accountable for your learning.

CHAPTER 3: TUTORS

Tutoring used to be only for the rich and famous, but that is not the case anymore. Today, the average Joe can afford to hire a tutor to teach anything. Usually tutors are used to help augment learning offered in a class setting. A tutor can come to your house, or you may decide to meet in a public location, or even at the tutor's home, to practice speaking, reading, listening, and/or writing Spanish. Tutors can help you with drills, explain confusing grammar points, proofread papers and assist with understanding assignments. Some tutors may even give their own assignments to challenge you to do more learning on your own.

Unlike classes or language schools, which have to spread their attention among so many students, tutors are a dedicated breed; they are willing to do what it takes to help you learn at your own pace. They can go as slowly as you want, or pick it up and go faster. It is important to have a plan going into any tutoring session or program. I would advise sitting down with your tutor to review and decide on some specifics before you begin to meet on a regular basis. Here are just a few points I would bring up with any prospective tutor:

1. Have a set start and end time in mind, and stick to it. It's important to respect the time that you and the tutor are dedicating to each session. That means turn your cell phone off, tell family and friends that you are unavailable for that hour, and find a quiet place to concentrate. Your tutor will appreciate not having his or her time wasted! (Even if you are paying by the hour, don't allow the tutor to feel that he could spend his talents helping other more motivated students.)

2. Be specific with your tutor. Know exactly what you want to learn and by when. This will help the tutor to plan learning activities while considering your allotted time, and preserve your money. Time and time again, I see students throw money at a tutor each week with no real goal in mind. There is no end point, and no assessment or determination as to when a student will no longer need the tutor's services. You need to have an idea of what you want your tutor to spend time on and do each week.

3. Meet at least once a week, although two or more times a week provides more reinforcement. Learning a language requires practice. The more often you have to practice the language and overcome obstacles and challenges, the better off you will be with the language. As a bare minimum, you should meet for a couple of hours once a week, because different kinds of practice and exposure are so important to learning the language well. With a great tutor, in a two-hour session you can expect to do any — and maybe all — of the following: a brief review, some chatting in Spanish, listening comprehension practice (perhaps a video), going over any problems and issues you've been having, some guided practice, perhaps some reading and writing, some more discussion, perhaps some games or puzzles in Spanish... and don't forget to schedule a five-minute break in there about halfway through.

4. Determine the cost. If you want a tutor for an hour, set up a per hour cost and stick to it. If a tutor charges a certain

rate per hour, ask them what you will get for your money. They should be able to detail activities and their plans for assisting you with learning Spanish. Find out how they conduct assessments, and how frequently. This will help you to know if you are learning, and help you measure how much you are learning and how quickly you are picking up the language. Ask them how they use the data from assessments to inform their teaching plans.

5. Be on time and be prepared. If your tutor has scheduled a specific time and place, make sure you do everything possible to be there on time. Students should respect their tutor's time and skills. Of course, tutors who assign homework want to see you reach your goals, so help them help you by completing all assignments on time. Write down any questions or problems you have while doing the work, and make sure you bring those notes to your next session.

If you adhere to the five points above, you will have a more enjoyable, cost-effective tutoring session. Tutors do not exist to do your work for you. They can help you do the work by breaking up concepts into smaller chunks which will help you understand more easily. Don't misunderstand the purpose of a tutor, which is to facilitate learning and help augment your Spanish abilities. Treat them with respect. They are there to be your friend. They are there to do a job for you. To avoid any awkward situations, you will want to keep this in perspective.

CHAPTER 4: CONVERSATIONAL GROUPS

Most major cities will have a Spanish conversation group (*grupo de conversación en español*) which you can join. Phoenix, my hometown, has one such group that meets every Saturday at the downtown Starbucks. Check out the Yellow Pages under "organizations" or do a web search for groups in your area. Sometimes you can find these groups by scanning local newspapers or independent community news circulars. If you attend a school, check to see if there is a club or group focusing on Spanish. When I was in college, I joined one. Besides getting to meet other people who share the same goal of learning Spanish, you get to meet Spanish-speakers in your community. You'll also have the opportunity to attend events that are culturally specific to Spanish. Our club helped a local library conduct some guided tours in Spanish when they had recently remodeled. It not only gave back to the community, but it was a good way for students to gain experience using the language in the real world.

These groups meet regularly and speak Spanish. They often chit-chat about family, work, friends, politics, social and community happenings, and much more. Often, these groups will plan outings to see a film, go to a book reading, and depending on where you live in, there may be many more interesting Spanish-related things to do.

These groups are a great way to practice the language with others who are learning the language or wanting to maintain the language once they have learned it. You will make friends (amigos) who have a similar interest in learning Spanish. Perhaps with these new friends you can do more practicing outside of the group activities. Be open to new opportunities and make yourself available to them!

If by chance you live in a rural area or a small town that does not have such a group, consider starting one yourself. You can advertise in the local newspaper or circular, and arrange to meet at the library, a coffee shop or a local park each week at a specific time. Make the advertisement as inviting as possible by mentioning that people need not be expert Spanish-speakers, unless you want it to be exclusive. Make it a relaxed environment where people can feel free to make linguistic mistakes. The most important aspect of the group should be to give everyone an opportunity to practice and use the language outside of a classroom, in a stress-free and comfortable environment. Have fun!

CHAPTER 5: BOOKS

Learning Spanish will require that you get some books (*libros*). You can learn anything you want by reading a book. The best books are chock full of information and carefully designed in ways that will help you learn. Despite the standard Spanish books that talk about grammar and vocabulary, you will also find bilingual books that have both the English and Spanish versions on opposite pages (those are called "bilateral translations"). There are workbooks to help you with practicing Spanish grammar rules and verb tenses. You will find newspapers (*periódicos*) and magazines (*revistas*) that are all in Spanish, and so much more!

Over the years, I've acquired numerous books on Spanish, Spanish translation, teaching Spanish and the like. I have workbooks, textbooks, dictionaries, encyclopedias, phrase books, teaching aids, fiction and non-fiction in Spanish. These books are great -- as long as you use them. The problem many beginning Spanish learners often run into is deciding which books to get. Trial and error is one way to go -- you will definitely encounter some books that are better than others. There are some books that I find particularly helpful and resourceful, although you may not share the same viewpoint. That's okay -- we are all made differently and like different things. The important thing is to have some criteria in mind when you are trying to decide what books to acquire. Following are some ideas that may help you.

I have sorted books into three categories: reference, teaching, and practice. Let's go through each of these types of books.

Reference

Reference books are resource tools such as dictionaries, thesauruses, encyclopedias, idiom books and phrase books. By definition, these books are good for looking things up, but don't offer much help in the realm of practice. For beginners, I find a good picture-themed book is helpful. Often you may not know the word in English (*inglés*), but if you see a picture with the Spanish word, that will help you learn it.

You can find relatively inexpensive Spanish-English dictionaries at just about any bookstore. Just page through any of them to select the one that will meet your needs. For my purposes, I start by considering ones that have the most words. I always feel I am getting more for my money when the dictionary contains more words than another. Then, look up a few words that you are interested in, and make sure those words appear in the dictionary. Read through the book to figure out if the definitions are helpful. Also, decide if you are interested in any extra "features" beyond just definitions. For example, some dictionaries include past tense forms of verbs; some dictionaries have sample sentences including the word you're looking up; some contain lists of idioms.

Try looking for a Spanish-English thesaurus. They are great for supplying synonyms, and they are quite handy for reports and papers.

I would also recommend getting a book containing idiomatic expressions. These can be hard to find in your average bookstore. As noted above, you may sometimes find idioms in your dictionary, but a book dedicated to idioms and phrases alone is very worth having. These books of idioms are priceless when it comes to everyday speech. What? You don't know what an idiom is? Don't worry. All of us probably use them every day, and often without knowing it. Idioms are simple expressions that have different meanings than what they mean literally. For example, in English, we use the idiom "I'll sleep on it" to mean "I'll take some time to think about it before making a decision." But if someone in Spanish was to say *Lo consultaré con la almohada*, you would probably think they are crazy in wanting to talk to a pillow – and they don't literally want to talk to a pillow! That's the Spanish equivalent of "I'll sleep on it." All languages have idioms and some can sound very strange to a foreigner. Having these books can come in very handy when you need to find just the right expression, and want to sound more accomplished in the language.

Instruction

In the "instruction" category I include textbooks, study aids, and grammar and vocabulary books. There are tons of these books on the market, and as always, some are better than others. Since teaching is very particular as to the type of learner you are, I cannot recommend specific books that would be good for everyone. My suggestion is to go to your local bookstore and review the various Spanish instruction books. See which ones "speak to you" (another idiom!) the most. They often range from more picture-based to more text-based books. I try to move towards those that will cover all aspects of grammar and are not heavy on vocabulary. You can use other sources to gain vocabulary, but the main function for an instruction type of book is to teach me something I didn't know before, regarding how the language works.

Practice

The purpose of these books is to help you get comfortable with using the language by practicing it over and over again, whether you're reading, writing, or speaking Spanish. The "practice" category contains workbooks, bilingual books, fiction and non-fiction, and magazines in Spanish. Reading and understanding is an incredibly important aspect of learning a language. I am afraid that with the ever increasing conversation-based training and Spanish education, the reading and comprehension-based learning will decrease, or fall to the wayside. Skipping over the important component of doing a lot of reading will just hurt people who are trying to learn the language. For beginners, I recommend *Easy Spanish Reader: A Three-Part Text for Beginning Students* by William T. Tardy, which I have used with many of my students. It takes some familiar things and expands on them. It starts out very easy, with one-to two-page stories, and then as the book progresses, each story gets a little longer. It's perfect for beginners and it's not intimidating at all.

Visit your local bookstore and go to their foreign language section. Collections of books in Spanish will usually be the largest of the foreign languages in that section, as many people want to learn Spanish for many reasons. Consider visiting bookstores when traveling in other countries. I've purchased a monolingual Spanish dictionary which is the Spanish equivalent to our English dictionary, and is great for enhancing your vocabulary and comprehension. I've also acquired an encyclopedia for my collection, as well as many other useful books to help me learn the culture and many aspects of the language. But if you cannot afford to buy these books, you're still in good hands. Your local library has many books you can check out and read. As you get better with your Spanish, you'll want to graduate to books and magazines that are only in Spanish. Reading what other Spanish-speakers read on a regular basis will be interesting for you, and challenging. It's a great way to develop and maintain your language abilities.

CHAPTER 6: TRAVELING

Have you ever heard the saying that the whole world is your classroom? It's true, or as we say in Spanish, *Es verdad*. You can travel anywhere and learn about cultures and peoples that are vastly different than your own. Traveling is the ultimate way to learn a new language. This is one of the reasons why total immersion classes are so popular -- because they make sense. Say, for example, someone pushes you out of an airplane and you parachute into another country where they speak a language you know nothing about, and no one speaks English. You have no phone, no access to the Internet, nothing but the clothes on your back. You would be forced to live with the first group you laid eyes on, at least until you were able to gather your resources and move on. If you decided to stay with that first group of people, I am certain that in time, you would slowly learn about them, their ways, and their customs. You would slowly start to communicate -- perhaps with hand gestures at first -- then move on to simple words and build up from there. If you were to stay longer, I'm sure you would become an important part of their society. This is the premise behind total immersion -- being completely surrounded by a language and the people who speak that language creates an insistent need for you to learn the language. Through context, hand gestures, sounds, and body language, you will be able to interpret what is being said, asked, and commanded in that language.

It can seem intimidating and I assure you, shy people will find this very difficult because it takes you out of your comfort zone. But it will be worth it. You will experience new sounds, new tastes, and new concepts that you never would have thought possible. It's easy to sit back and assume everyone around the world does the same thing as you already do, acts the same way and lives their life the same as we do in the United States. That is actually one of the reasons why the U.S. is not highly regarded in terms of knowing other cultures and languages. It is easy to sit back and judge others when we are in the safety and comfort of our own homes, far from many challenges other people face day to day.

I have done a lot of traveling, by myself and in groups, and there are pluses and minuses to both. The obvious negatives of group travel are: you adhere to group schedules instead of doing and seeing what you want; you're spoon-fed only the information given to groups without being able to explore, see, and experience things first-hand; and you don't get to really know the culture, the people, or the language because you are surrounded by a group of people just like you -- your own "safety zone" away from home. These are the hindrances of group travel. You may get a great rate, but what's the "opportunity cost"? You will sacrifice a lot of interacting with the locals. You will be talked to death by tour guides who will only give you their version of what they want you to know. You will miss out on asking various "local" people what their thoughts and viewpoints are. And of course, with groups, you will have delays, schedule changes, and things you may or may not do because you are in a group setting.

For those and other reasons, my preference is to travel alone. It forces me to keep my wits about me and challenges me to interact more with the local population. If you are dependent on local people to guide you, provide your information, and provide help and services, you will use the language more. Ultimately, that is really what you want. You want to use the language in a natural environment away from the clinical stuffiness of a classroom or arbitrary recording. Language lives and is alive because of the people who go out and use it daily.

From climbing to the top of the tallest pyramid in the western hemisphere to getting around one of the largest cities of the world, there is nothing like tackling that challenge alone. Your mind becomes more open and more active because you are constantly trying to interpret and decipher what things mean and why things are the way they are. You are paying close attention for your own protection and survival in whatever place you're visiting. Being open to interactions on your travels is also a wonderful way to get to know the people, real people, who live there -- their families and histories are all there. From a teacher in Guatemala who wears a wedding ring even though she is not married because she wants to keep men away from her, to a homeless man sitting in a pew at church next to a well-dressed and perhaps a well-to-do family, you will observe and perhaps become a part of some wonderful examples of life, of a living culture. You get to experience many unique situations and encounter many wonderful people firsthand when you travel.

Traveling may not be for everyone, and that's understandable. There is a lot to plan, not to mention the expense and safety issues. For men, traveling can be relatively safe, but women have additional concerns they should consider when traveling alone. As a bare minimum, review any government advisory notifications before your trip. Travel guides is another wonderful place to learn of safe places to visit.

If you are planning a trip, you will want to spend some time contemplating various aspects of your travels. You need to plan around a good time of year to visit your destination. You need to save up money to buy tickets or pay for a way to get there. You need to come up with some way to live there, eat, and have money available to take advantage of activities during the days and enjoy the nights.

First you must research how much all that will cost you. Determine if you can be flexible about your travel time. Keep in mind that you will often have cheaper airfare and other travel costs if you travel outside peak days (often Fridays through Mondays). You can usually barter in other countries -- especially in Latin America -- which can save you some money. Barter for cab rides, barter for souvenirs and much more! It can be fun, and it is legitimately a part of the culture.

Here are some tips to help make traveling easier, better and more enjoyable, and to help you avoid any potential disasters:

Take some of your cash (after you exchange it for the local currency) and hide it on you in an inconspicuous place like a sock, a shoe, a bra -- someplace close to your body that cannot be easily ripped off. That way, if you do run into danger and you are forced to give your money away, you will still have some money in a secure place. The amount of money that you keep safe should be enough to help you go someplace safe and provide you with any emergency necessities like food and drink.

Travel light, as much as possible. It's okay to bring a suitcase, but don't bring any more than one. I'd suggest one suitcase and one day bag, whether that is a small backpack or camera case. I would refrain from using a suitcase on wheels as your day bag, since you may encounter multiple obstacles such as stairs, cobblestoned streets, curbs or other annoyances which will make wheeling your luggage more aggravating than helpful. Carry something light and be mindful of how much weight you will carry throughout the day of walking. You don't want a lot to carry when you are touring museums, shops and eateries all day long. (Of course, when you go into museums, they are usually going to make you check any big bags that you have – but some museums don't even do that. For example, the Metropolitan Museum of Art in New York City doesn't permit you to carry bags, and they don't have a bag check. You should find out the rules before you go!) Extra bags create more to keep track of and lug around. Keep it simple and you will have a more enjoyable time.

Bring a couple types of clothes with you that you can mix and match to make new outfits. Since I'm a guy, it's pretty easy for me. I just pack a couple pairs of jeans, a pair of slacks, socks, shoes and some different tops (from t-shirts to polo and button-down shirts). Women can bring a couple of skirts, shorts and slacks with some versatile tops. Be respectful of visiting religious sites. They often require more conservative dress – nothing showing the shoulders or legs. Remember that Americans dress very casually than other countries. That can get misinterpreted as disrespectful or inconsiderate. Show your visiting country that you can be a respectful American tourist in what you wear as well as how you behave.

Make sure your shoes are comfortable. If you buy new shoes for the trip, wear them long enough to break them in before you leave for the trip. I remember one trip to Ireland when I wore a pair of brand new, two-week-old walking shoes. They rubbed against the side of my little toe on my right foot. After a couple of days walking many hours, my toe was not only swollen, but it began to affect my knee and my lower back. I had to buy a knee brace and eventually, stop wearing the shoes. It really affected my mobility. When you travel, your mobility is the one thing you don't want to interfere with! By the time I realized that it was in fact the shoes that were the problem, the damage had already been done. Don't get surprised on your trip. Wear shoes you have worn for a few weeks, at least.

Having a limited set of outfit combinations will make traveling easier. You may ask, "what if I spill something on my outfit?" or "What if I sweat a lot?" Don't worry! There are usually laundry facilities that can clean your dirty clothes while you are out and about sightseeing during the day. Use them. They are cheap and save you having to wash when you are wiped out and tired from a long day walking and touring. They are well worth the expense, and don't cost very much.

Before your trip, research some events or activities you think you'll enjoy. Go online to find out if there are any special events happening during your trip. Don't plan every waking moment, but plan to see or do a few things each day. Select the experiences you really want to try first, and then if you run out of time or something happens that does not allow you to see the rest, you won't be too disappointed. This helps to free up your time so you can stop and smell those roses more; have a chat with a local about something you're seeing or doing; or check out something interesting where you are. You push timetables each and every day of your working life. You shouldn't have to do that when you are traveling for fun.

Smile and say hello. You're much more inviting to approach and speak to if you are wearing a smile and you say hello to people you cross paths with. It's a great way to start a conversation, or get valuable information, tips, tricks, and help when you need it. It is said that a smile will help you live longer and make your chitter-chatter more pleasant to the ear. It has something to do with the small muscles in your voice box that change the resonance of your tone of voice.

Try to make the best of any bad situations that occur. The better you get at doing this, the more you will enjoy yourself and the experience. Bad things may happen -- that's part of life. But how you handle your behavior, by not having things get you down and frustrated, will make things work out much more smoothly. View the glass as half full, not half empty, when you go through a difficult experience. I know it is easier said than done, but realize that situations can improve if you are in a better mindset. Panicking and raising your voice will not do anything to help most situations, and will actually often do the opposite of what you want, by making others agitated and unwilling or unable to help you or the situation. Stay calm, take a few deep breaths, and observe. Only speak if the words coming out of your mouth will help resolve the situation at hand.

Once when I was in Mexico with a couple of friends, we visited a historical building that happened to house multiple political offices as well as a police station. The building contained some interesting art. While we were inside, a crowd formed quickly right outside the only exit to the building, shouting and in an uproar over some injustice. All we knew is that we were trapped in the building, as the crowd had blocked the doorway. They did not look like they were going to budge at all. For almost anyone, it would have been a perfect moment to panic, get worried, throw your hands up or quiver in a corner and cry, but I stayed calm. I saw the entrance to the police station and walked right in. I explained our predicament to them and asked for their help. A group of officers came out and opened a pathway by pushing the crowd back. Their quick thinking and action allowed us to leave safely. The moral of the story is to stay calm when times are tough. It helps clear your mind so you can consider your options and take immediate action.

My final recommendation to you is keep an open mind. When you travel and experience different perspectives and cultures unlike your own, you will see, hear and witness things that may seem strange and weird. Don't dismiss them so quickly. Challenge yourself to keep your mind open and try to view things from another perspective. Ask questions to get to know more about what it is they are doing or why they believe that way. Become a world learner. Be one who is open to new experiences and does not pass judgment on things when they do not know the whole story. You may know your truth about what you are seeing from your own beliefs, background and education, but you do so with a limited view of others' beliefs, backgrounds and educations. This will help you become a better communicator, a better person, and a better traveler.

PART 2: GET YOUR GEEK ON

CHAPTER 7: TECHNOLOGY

Technology has come a long way since I started to learn Spanish. I did not have the Internet, smartphones, or computers. In fact, compact discs were just starting to get popular when I was in school. Today there is such a wide variety of technology out there that it can make your head spin. What should you get? What is the best device available? Which software programs should you download or buy? There are so many choices – and it's enough to handle just learning Spanish without having to make these decisions too. That is why this second half of the book is devoted to technology and all things digital. I'm assuming you may not know everything that's out there and if you do, please forgive me. This information will help people who have a hard time with technology, and tech-savvy people can skim this section just in case I mention something they may not have heard.

By technology, I am referring to computers (*computadoras*), the Internet, audio files, video files, CDs, DVDs, software programs and apps for computers, laptops, e-readers, smartphones and tablets. If you don't own or you don't have access to any of these things, consider investing in some technology to help you on your road to bilingualism. Since technology is becoming almost indispensable these days, it is important to know what is out there that can help you learn faster and be better prepared. Just about every home in the United States owns and uses a computer of some sort. Whether that is a desktop computer, a smartphone, a laptop, or a tablet, computers are becoming a necessity in today's society. Chances are you will find yourself using some form of technology soon if you aren't doing so already.

Technology doesn't have to be intimidating. Embrace it. Think of it as a tool to help make your life easier. Cars take you from point A to point B. Dishwashers help save you time in the kitchen. There are so many things we have today that make our lives easier and more manageable. Take the washing machine from the mid-nineteenth century, for example. Prior to its invention, you had to wash each piece of clothing by hand in soap and water, then rinse it out and hang it on a clothesline to dry. These machines have revolutionized the way people do laundry and how they live. Computers and technological devices also help make our lives better. If used wisely, they are a great asset to anyone's home and life.

However, I would like to caution you about the over-use of technology. Some people hide behind technology to avoid living their lives. You might think it is easier to hide behind sending emails in Spanish and watching videos, but it will be so much more fulfilling if you try to use your new language skills in the real world. Explore the vastness that is our planet. You will learn a lot by getting out of your shell and meeting people and experiencing all life has to offer. Never forget: technology is a tool for you to make learning Spanish easier, faster and better. If you view it in the right light, you will go far in mastering this language.

CHAPTER 8: AUDIO

We'll start out small by talking about something small: audio files. Audio files come in many formats: CDs, MP3s, and wavs are a few of the file types.

CDs (compact discs) are the actual physical objects – the round silver discs -- that store the audio files you play in a CD player. This is getting to be old school; however, many cars still have CD players and many language companies still produce language CDs for use in cars, on computers, and other places that you have CD players. The main purpose of an audio file is to hear the language as you would normally hear it -- in the real world. Language discs typically have a little bit of instruction followed by sentences for you to listen to and repeat. Some will even ask you questions in Spanish and give you time to respond in Spanish. Still others will provide you with a workbook or textbook of some kind, which contain exercises and other helpful aids such as pictures to facilitate learning. Obviously, the car-only language learning discs will focus on learning the language by listening and repeating. Please do not read and drive! (You want to live long enough to enjoy your Spanish skills, don't you?)

If you can, you might find it better to rip the discs onto a computer using one of the many audio file formats such as

MP3 or wav files. I have used both formats and do not find one more convenient than the other. Of course there are some good language programs on disc, in addition to some poor ones. Shop carefully. Read customer reviews and take them to heart. If you do not see a lot of reviews for a product, pass it by or do more searching on the product to find more reviews. I recommend programs that offer more conversational dialogue to help you to develop your comprehension, as opposed to programs that only have you repeat back sentences. You will make more progress if you can expand your understanding of the language, instead of just repeating phrases and sentences aloud.

Another benefit to audio files is portability. Some newer cars have USB ports where you can plug in a flash or jump drive and play your MP3s. Other devices allow you to download your MP3s and play them. Even if you focus on just listening to what is being said in Spanish, you will be helping yourself to the sound and "feel" of the language.

Many websites contain audio files you can click on to hear a native Spanish speaker. You may even find audio files as streaming content. Podcasts are audio files that you can download to your computer or listen to directly on a website. Click on them -- the more you are exposed to and hear Spanish, the better and easier it will be for you as you venture into the real world with your Spanish. Listening comprehension is a very important component to learning Spanish. Communication requires a receiver (listener) and a transmitter (talker). You can't have one without the other, and your skills need to be developed in both for you to know the language. Don't shy away from audio files -- they're a good thing!

CHAPTER 9: WEBSITES

The Internet is a frontier that constantly renews itself, with new content and new things to see and do each day. If you were to enter the phrase "learn Spanish" on a web search engine, you would get millions of results within mere seconds of pressing "enter." The best way to find the right Spanish learning content on the web is to narrow your search keywords. My tip for you is to use books such as grammar books or textbooks to help limit your search words. Use the index section of the book, which will list the various grammatical parts of speech and language. Use those same words to use to search as your keywords when you need some help or more information, or a different way to learn about them. For example, you might want to search for "Spanish preterite vs. imperfect" or "Spanish subjunctive" – a couple of grammatical sticking points that lots of learners often need to review, or need help with.

The Internet has many different resources that can help you learn Spanish. There are blogs, forums, grammar lessons, podcasts, social sites, pen pal sites, games and activity sites, stories and much more! Here is a brief description of each of these types of sites:

Blog is short for "web log." It's almost like a diary or journal, and very often it has a theme, and focuses on one topic of the writer's choice. Individual people will write about a topic and post it on a webpage for others to read and comment on. If you find blogs written in Spanish, this will help you with your reading and comprehension skills. If you comment on the blog using Spanish, it will help your writing skills. Blogs are wonderful because they can provide glimpses of culture and real life adventure, conflict and strife. They offer a very human component to a normally monotonous task of learning the grammatical parts of a language.

Forums are sites set up to answer questions or to hold discussions on specific subjects. There are some sites where you can ask questions about Spanish, or ask questions in Spanish about culture or anything else. People will post responses in the same place. These are called threads and a thread holds one topic, one question, or one discussion. It's a great way to have your voice heard, and hear others, about a variety of issues. They are a wonderful place to get your Spanish questions answered.

Grammar lesson sites will, of course, explain the grammar of a language, including everything from nouns to verbs, subjunctive to indicative, active to passive, and the list goes on. The grammar sites will provide a clear explanation of each grammar theme and some examples to help drive home the point. Some sites will give you quizzes or practice drills to help reinforce the grammatical concepts.

As we noted in the previous chapter, podcasts are a type of audio file that can cover many themes and topics. Some podcasts provide video, but audio-only is more common. Sites that provide grammar lessons or sell you products to help with learning Spanish will often have podcasts to entice you to use their site often. Podcasts will be posted on a regular basis – often daily, weekly, or monthly. The most common ones will have weekly or monthly updates. Some devices or computer programs will allow you to download podcasts and monitor when new ones have been posted.

Social sites, or social media sites, are Internet places like Facebook, Goodreads, Meetup, or Google+. They allow you to establish a profile and connect with the world. You can use such sites to chat with Spanish-speaking people around the world. LinkedIn is another great social site that has "Groups" you can join related to Spanish. Some of them also serve the same purpose as forums do, and you can connect with many people who share the same interests as you.

Pen pal sites are wonderful places to interact one-on-one with someone who speaks Spanish. Usually, you post your profile and browse other people's profiles. If you can contact someone who wants to learn English, they might be helpful with your Spanish in return. You would write to them in Spanish and they would correspond back in English. I have used these sites and you can develop some great friendships. However, you shouldn't be disappointed if the friendship doesn't last very long – it happens when it turns out you might not actually have so much in common with the other person, and then you'd run out of things to talk about together. As always on the Internet, there's some possible danger of someone learning too much about you and causing you some harm. It's always good to be cautious with your private information on the Internet.

Games and activity sites are leisure sites that help to support your language learning. You can find crossword puzzles, word searches, and many other grammatical and vocabulary sites that will help reinforce your studies. They are a great way to relax and enjoy learning a language. Use them to supplement other learning methods you're reading about in this book.

Story sites provide short stories or even full-length novels in Spanish. These are fiction (the non-fiction sites tend to be blogs). This is a good way to relax and improve your reading skills. Some sites will have comprehension questions at the end. Others may have ways for you to comment and offer suggestions, or perhaps you'll be able to post your own stories to share.

Of course, the Internet is a great place to find videos in Spanish, which do two things to help increase your learning. First, they provide you a visual context for what you're hearing.

For example, if you see someone entering a store and start talking to the clerk, you will gain some visual clues as to what the person might be discussing or asking. You can view the surroundings, make observations about a culture, and witness an event through video. The other benefit is audio comprehension. You will hear the language being spoken aloud in a natural way. Some videos will be scripted and can come off as made-up or unrealistic. YouTube and the BBC channel are great sites to find videos in Spanish.

Use the Internet to help you learn Spanish. It's one of the greatest technologies we have and it is ever increasing in its capabilities and depth of content.

CHAPTER 10: SOFTWARE

Computer software programs have been around many years. While you usually would purchase the program from either a website or store (and bookstores tend to sell this software in their foreign language section), you can sometimes find free downloads. After the program is installed on your computer, you can run it to find interactive activities such as games, stories and video, and you learn vocabulary, grammar and comprehension. More sophisticated programs will link you to a website for more video and gaming content. The more expensive programs are very often better quality than the cheaper ones that you will find on the market. "You get what you pay for" comes to mind – though sometimes, you will find something unexpected!

They all assert that you will learn Spanish quickly and easily using their system or method. Many programs contain workbooks or study guides as part of the purchase price, which can be helpful for you to write Spanish away from the computer. Some activities in the workbook go hand in hand with what you do in the program. And some programs will offer audio discs you can use in a car, computer, or another portable device. While these supplemental study materials can be neat features, I believe they do not necessarily help in the learning process. You should question whether purchasing a software program just for these features is worth the price when compared to a good Spanish resource book or audio-only program.

A downside to using software programs is they can make you feel isolated. If you are introverted and are happy to be by yourself, then this is a wonderful way to get exposure to the language. Learning Spanish by yourself does not necessarily help you as much as learning in a more social context does, though. You will not know when you make mistakes and what you should do to correct them, and this may leave you somewhat frustrated and annoyed. You also run the risk of adopting poor pronunciation habits. A few programs may offer voice recognition technology to analyze your voice patterns while you speak and provide you with information about whether you've given correct or incorrect responses, and this information can be quite helpful -- as long as it is accurate. You will need to have a critical eye and ear when it comes to using software programs.

My recommendation is to use software programs sparingly. They can be great ways to start up a conversation or comprehension game with a Spanish tutor or teacher. Having an actual person work with you through a software program is the best scenario. You will have the feedback you need to improve your skills. Plus the software program can provide multiple ways to surround yourself with the language and provide material and activities to do.

CHAPTER 11: RADIO

Sound waves have influenced humanity since the time that cavemen were banging clubs and making music. In fact, one of the most common learning styles is even called "auditory." Some people pick things up quicker if they listen to instructions, a lecture, a language, or an audio-book. They can retain the information longer and produce it quicker than just by reading it, for example. Now I'm not saying these people are super-human and this is the best possible way to learn Spanish. I am just stating that for some people, listening enhances and increases their chances of doing something well. And certainly, when you're learning Spanish, even if "auditory" is not your main learning style – it's very important to listen!

Radio is a perfect way to pick up Spanish. It will teach you new vocabulary, a people's culture, and increase your comprehension of the language. It is often more challenging because you don't have body language or visual clues to help make quick connections about what's being communicated. Your ears have to do all the work by picking up auditory cues, expressions, sound effects, intonation, as well as the words themselves, to have a clear understanding.

If you live far from Spanish-speaking countries, cities, towns, or people, chances are you may not have a radio station dedicated to Spanish. If you are one of the lucky ones, you may have more than one station to choose from. Don't forget to check your AM dial too. You may find some interesting talk-radio programs in Spanish there.

I happen to be one of the lucky ones who live in a large city that has a multitude of Spanish-speakers. There are many stations that broadcast in Spanish and I can pick my favorites, and I can listen whether I'm at home, or in my car driving. Some companies will allow you to listen to the radio as you work; you can give this a shot, but don't jeopardize your job just to learn Spanish using the radio. If you can do this, however, more power to you!

For all you unluckier ones, turn to the Internet. Many smartphones have apps that allow you to listen to Internet radio. You can also access various radio stations through your desktop or laptop computers. This is an excellent way to hear Spanish spoken in various regions of the world; try using the search words "Spanish radio stations streaming" (without the quotation marks when you put the words in the search box) and you should get lots of options of Spanish-language stations to listen to live! Stations come in many varieties such as talk, discussion or music.

I suggest finding stations outside the country. This will do two things for you. First, you will become acquainted with various Spanish dialects. Dialects are the way that languages are spoken regionally, so for example, in the U.S., Bostonians and Southerners seem to speak differently from each other. The first advantage of learning various dialects permits you familiarity with the sound and rhythm, and that in turn helps you to feel more confident speaking Spanish to a larger audience. Second, it will increase your comprehension levels. You will learn more about the regions you are listening. Perhaps a discussion on local art, local destinations, local current events or the national news in that country will pique your interest in something you enjoy. It might just make that connection that prompts you to want to learn more on the topic. Since culture and language are so interconnected, by understanding one, it will help you with understanding the other.

If you are like me, you gather U.S. and world news either over TV, the radio or some other sort of news outlet (paper, online or otherwise). You know what the big stories are, here and elsewhere. Depending upon how much information is pumped to you daily, you may know it frontwards and backwards. Often listening to information from other countries provides you with a different slant, different stories (maybe some that are more localized to the area), more nationalized (from their point of view), and possibly more challenging to you. If you are trying to understand a news story that is in a local town, there is a very good chance it was not announced to you through one of the English-speaking news outlets. Therefore it is new to you! You will be more interested in figuring out what they are saying, what has happened, and what people are doing about the situation.

Don't just listen to talk radio only! Check out the various Spanish and Latin beats too. There's samba, rumba, tango, salsa, and so much more. The lyrics to songs you may enjoy hearing can help you understand Spanish too. Music can make everything more enjoyable and less stressful, because as we know, learning works better when your environment is fun. You are more motivated because you are getting into the beat, the words, the person singing or the instruments playing.

Besides the obvious lack of the visual, there is one other downside to the radio. Some people's hearing focuses on specific sounds. For example, one person may recall every lyric to every song they hear after a few times. Another person may know a few words of the lyrics, but not enough to sing the song. This second person may be focusing more on the instruments and how they are producing the sounds behind the words. If you focus more on how the music sounds or is played and not on the lyrics or words sung, your comprehension will not improve as quickly. Don't waste time thinking the radio will increase your learning by leaps and bounds if you focus more on the music. I caution you on this because I am one of those people who listen and enjoy rich, melodic pieces. If the notes combine to form an incredible melody, I am hooked on how it sounds and what the artist does with it rather than what the singer is saying. For me to learn a language, I cannot use radio as a significant source.

CHAPTER 12: TELEVISION

Like radio, television is an incredible way to transport yourself into the Spanish culture, but in a more complete way. With this method, you will have visuals to back up the sounds you hear. You will be able to see what is happening (context) and hear how it is going down. But if you live in an area with very few Spanish-speaking people, you won't have a local station in Spanish. Larger cities will most likely have Spanish-only stations such as Telemundo, Univisión, and Galavisión because that tends to be where you will find large populations of Spanish-speakers. So also like radio, for those of you who are lucky enough to live in or near a large city, you may have access to a Spanish channel. For all others, your best bet is the Internet, satellite or cable. Again, some smartphones will have apps that allow you to view television channels from around the world. You can also go online and check out video clips from television stations around the world.

On one of my visits to Mexico, I got hooked on a *telenovela* (the Spanish version of a soap opera). Each day, I made sure that I was back at my hotel room in time to catch the next episode. To me, the characters felt real. I cared about them and what happened to them. I cried, laughed, and shouted "Oh no!" during shocking moments. Start browsing for Spanish shows you'll enjoy watching. With cultural differences, you won't find the exact same types of shows, but you will find good movies, sitcoms, dramas and variety shows. If you are traveling to a Spanish-speaking country, turn on the television and see what's on the various channels. Find out what locals believe is worth watching by asking for their favorite shows. Asking for recommendations is probably a great way to start a conversation. You might even find that same show online or re-playing on your local Spanish-speaking TV station at home. A few years after that trip to Mexico, when I had just moved to Phoenix, I came across that same *telenovela* here while channel surfing. I was able to enjoy it further and I even found out there was a sequel!

If you subscribe to Internet television channels, consider paying for a subscription to a Spanish-speaking one. Many digital devices that connect to televisions will stream your subscribed programming right to you. Go online to investigate the types of shows available and see if you can find clips to view -- and make sure you like the station before subscribing. Or subscribe and cancel if it turns out you don't care for the programming.

Another great way to take advantage of your television is to subscribe to a streaming service that includes movies, such as Netflix or Blockbuster. These services will provide foreign films which you can stream and enjoy.

Television will help increase your vocabulary and comprehension, but don't depend on it alone. It is a passive medium and you will need more interactive methods if you want to learn Spanish well.

CHAPTER 13: APPS

Tablets, smartphones, some gaming devices and some televisions allow you to download small programs called apps, short for applications. These are handy little programs which keep you mobile. What I like about these programs is the fact that you can be stuck in a waiting room or on a bus, and pull up an app on your phone that can test your memory skills on vocabulary, or allow you to play a word game to occupy your time. There are apps for Spanish-English dictionaries, flashcards for vocabulary, interactive games, and video and audio clips for comprehension. Some will require a Wi-Fi connection to access the Internet, while others will be self-contained and accessible on the device alone.

I like to use apps for games and flashcards. Flashcards test and reinforce memory of vocabulary, sentences and phrases. Spanish newspaper articles will test my reading and comprehension skills. Most are free to download, but often times there will be a "pro" version that costs some money. These "pro" versions still provide the same content, but limit or remove pesky advertisements and allow you to do more like store and mark items or other things that are specific to that program.

One of the apps I enjoy using is Spanish Flashcards by Bradley G. Hohn. It's a free app which covers idioms, sentences, verbs and other vocabulary words, with translations that are between the Spanish from Spain and the English from the United Kingdom. There are many, many more free apps available. Just search your app store or marketplace.

For reading news articles, I like the program Titulares. You can view multiple media types, including newspapers, magazines and television. Everything in Titulares is in Spanish, from the instructions to the navigation buttons. However, be careful what you click on using this program, especially if you are just a beginner to Spanish: You can easily get into the settings and alter viewing and sound capabilities without fully understanding the wide-ranging effects in the app, which could then make navigating it a challenge.

Beginners (and also more advanced linguists) may enjoy the app called World Newspapers. You can pull up your favorite newspapers from other countries, and the buttons and instructions are all in English. As I think about which Spanish-speaking country I'd like to visit next, I tend to gravitate toward the country's local newspapers and magazines in order to understand their current events, culture, and activities. I might even come across an interesting place to check out or an event I might want to put on my "to-do" list. Right now, I am reading *El País* and *ABC*, two of Spain's national newspapers. Depending on your smartphone carrier, World Newspapers is available either free or at a nominal charge.

You can also use apps for to enhance your travels. I would recommend downloading a good converter app to change not only currency, but measurements (weights, length and volume). A good dictionary is another useful app. There are also translator apps available. (As I will caution you in the next chapter, you should be a bit careful of machine-generated translation apps.)

KEITH WALTERS

As with other technology, I do not recommend depending on apps as a sole source for learning Spanish, but rather a tool to help you along the way.

50

CHAPTER 14: DEVICES

Technology such as e-readers, hand-held machine-generating translators (and lots of miscellaneous gadgets not yet invented as of this writing -- but probably in development now) are super for assisting you in learning Spanish. Smartphones fall into this category too, because outside of apps, you can use much of a smartphone's functionality for learning Spanish.

Many models of smartphones have front-facing cameras that will allow you to video chat with someone face-to-face. If you use Skype, a webcam program to speak to people via the Internet, then this would benefit you. It not only will save you money on international calling charges, but it will allow you to develop friendships with Spanish-speakers outside your area. You can post your Skype ID online, requesting native Spanish-speakers to chat with you. Use it to improve fluency, obtain tutoring services or general assistance with the language. A lot about speaking to a native requires quick "think-on-your-feet" skills. If you don't know a specific word, try to talk around it, or describe the word. Perhaps the native speaker will see what you are doing and help provide the word you were intending to say. Or you can always ask, by saying *"¿Cómo se dice en español?"*

Used with desktop and laptop computers, webcams project your real-time image and sound to others -- depending on the availability of a microphone on the webcam. If other people have webcams, you'll be able to see them over the Internet too. Web sites such as Skype can download software to your computer which allows you to video chat with people around the world. You can search the web for other similar sites and programs so you can chat with a real person.

Not as popular as they once were, language translator devices, or what I referred to earlier as machine-generated translators, are small and portable. They often hold a certain amount of data and will supply words, phrases or sentences translated to and from English. However, languages are living entities, in that words, phrases or sentences may change over time. Nuances to meaning are difficult for machines to get right, and many words and phrases may have double or multiple meanings, all of which can render these machines somewhat unreliable. Depending upon the purpose, it could get you into trouble if the incorrect expression is used in the real world. I find these devices more of a crutch than a tool and do not recommend them.

E-readers permit reading books, magazines and newspapers electronically. It saves on buying books and storing them (and cutting down trees). These devices can hold thousands of books, and some can even read to you out loud using a computer-generated voice. You can play word games and so much more with them, and their portable size gives you the freedom to take anywhere. I use mine to save money and store books, newspapers and magazines in both English and Spanish. If you can purchase one, I would recommend it.

Finally, there are tablets, which are mini-computers, so to speak. They let you use software programs, apps, surf the web, watch television, listen to the radio, send email, and video chat with friends, and they are even more portable than laptops. Of course, I use them for games and reading in Spanish, as well as many other purposes. They really are great fun.

As I have suggested before in this book, don't rely on technology so much that it will prevent you from truly learning Spanish. If you must use it constantly to communicate (look up words, translate, etc.), you are not doing yourself any favors. Exercise your brain muscles and think, memorize, and evaluate Spanish. Try to be as interactive with the language as possible. For any introverts out there especially, this can be a real hang-up. Push yourself to get out into the real world and talk to people in Spanish. Live in the language. Even if you use technology to locate and find people to meet, force yourself to interact with people face to face (and in safe places). Use common sense and avoid people who seem shady. If your gut instinct gives you an uneasy feeling, then it is time to stop communications with that specific individual. Learn as much as you can from technology, but connect with some good people to help you excel in your Spanish language abilities.

PART 3: THE JACKPOT!

CHAPTER 15: TEN WAYS TO SPANISH FLUENCY

As a special bonus, I am including my top ten ways to improve your Spanish fluency. I don't want to say learning Spanish is easy and for some, it will be a challenge. You can do it, though! Millions of people learn other languages throughout the world. It is possible! And you can be one of those millions.

If you follow this top-ten list and do as much of it as you possibly can, with some effort, you will find your Spanish-using ability improve dramatically.

1. Take a class or hire a tutor to learn Spanish. Even if you did not do well in school, you can still learn the language with this hands-on approach. Besides getting the necessary feedback, it forces accountability onto you, the student. You will be held to a standard of producing and learning. You must prepare for each lesson, otherwise you'll be wasting money and time. This can be a great motivator. Give it a try.

2. Practice what you have learned each day for at least 30 minutes. Experts say that if you expose yourself a hundred times or more to a new word, grammar point, idiom, song or whatever, that you will truly have learned it. It will be integrated into your long term memory. If you read aloud, do verb drills, talk to your dog or cat, use a software program, play some interactive language games or something that forces you to use your brain in the other language, you're going to make great progress. I've had students post vocabulary cards throughout their home and physically move throughout their dwelling picking up things, sitting down, turning on and saying what they are doing – in Spanish – each step of the way. This commits names of objects to memory. As you try to remember words, you can recall your actions to help trigger the words you need. I even have soap (*jabón*), shampoo (*champú*) and conditioner (*condicionador*) dispensers labeled in Spanish the shower! This forces you to remember to use the language day in and day out.

3. Try to speak to people who know Spanish. Whether it's a passing greeting to a neighbor, a colleague at work, or someone you encounter during the day, say a few words (*palabras*) to them in Spanish. It may put a smile on their face and brighten their day -- as well as yours!

4. Watch television or video clips in Spanish. Dedicate a bit of time to watching a TV show in Spanish. Even if you do not understand anything that is being said, study the body language. See if you can get the gist of what is happening through what you see visually. If you do not have a station in your area in Spanish, go online in search of shows to watch.

5. Listen to Spanish on the radio. Spend driving time, exercise time, waiting room time or some other "down" time to listen to Spanish over the radio. Listen to Spanish music or a talk show. Again, you may not understand everything, or anything, but focus on listening for words you know. They may give you a clue to what is being discussed or sung. If you do not have a station in your area dedicated to Spanish-speakers, then check for an Internet radio station as an alternative.

6. Read magazines, newspapers or anything else written in Spanish. Some local grocery stores may have circulars in Spanish for jobs and classifieds. Check out the magazine rack too. Also, your local bookstore may have whole books written in Spanish. For you e-readers, search for books in Spanish you can purchase or borrow from the library for free. Pick out words you understand and see if you can piece the meaning together.

7. Search for Internet sites to visit for activities, lessons, games and much more in Spanish. The web has huge quantities of resources for you to learn Spanish. Surf leisurely and see what's available, and what you like to do.

8. Join a community Spanish club to practice your speaking and interaction skills. Check out your community center, the library, your local grocery store or conduct Internet searches to see if such a group exists in your area. If you do not find one, consider starting one. Put an ad on Craig's List, at your local grocery store, on meetup.com, in your local coffee shop or library, and start one up. You can do monthly activities together or meet weekly to chat.

9. Have dinner at a Spanish restaurant and order your meal in Spanish. Many communities have restaurants catering to various nationalities -- Spanish being one of them. Plan a meal there every now and then, and get to know the staff. Probably someone there speaks Spanish. Challenge yourself to order and conduct your entire visit in Spanish.

10. Plan a trip to a Spanish-speaking country. Foreign travel will open your adventurous side, and it can be thrilling to explore a new culture and people. It would be the perfect test to see how well you are learning Spanish. You could not ask for a better reward for all the hard work you have invested. Mark a date on your calendar, which can be a powerful motivator. *¡Buen viaje!*

If you make learning Spanish fun and exciting, you will stick with it longer and you will absorb the language faster. You will see your fluency improve. Your self-confidence will increase. Expose yourself to the language as much as possible. From this moment on, you will have passed the hilltop. The vast panorama and the enjoyment of the Spanish-speaking world is out there in all its glory. With all these hurdles behind you, you have the knowledge to advance with Spanish, its cultures, people and a whole new world to explore. You have the capability -- now go and make it happen for yourself, today!

CHAPTER 16: FINDING YOUR LEARNING STYLE

As you get ready to learn Spanish, one of the most important things you can do to prepare yourself is to find out your learning style. "Learning style" is a term that encompasses various ways or approaches to learning, and your best learning style is the best way for you to learn new things. Everyone does not learn best the same way, and that's one of the distinctions that make us unique as individuals. Good teachers often teach to quite a few different learning styles. Unfortunately, if a teacher is utilizing a learning style that does not benefit you, you may find it difficult to grasp the concept being taught. Knowing exactly what your learning style is will be important as you select from the multitude of ways to practice and learn Spanish from this book. Once you can identify your learning style, you can go back through the various chapters and select methods tailored to how you learn best.

I will walk you through each of the different learning styles and what they entail. There are a multitude of learning theories out there. This book just touches on a couple. I encourage you to research other learning styles or MIT (multiple intelligences). I'm sure you will find a plethora of interesting pieces of research out there. At the end of this chapter, I will provide you with a couple of resources to identify your own learning style. Educators have studied how people learn for decades. One such model was developed by Bernice McCarthy, and is called 4MAT. In that model, the learners are divided into four different types of learners: imaginative, analytical, common sense, and dynamic.

Imaginative learners are people who think of the question word "why?" and try to pursue the answers to this question. They watch, listen, and share their ideas with those around them. Group studies and classroom discussions are places in which imaginative learners thrive.

Analytical learners try to answer the question word "what?" Facts and details are king when learning new material and concepts. Lectures are great ways for analytical learners to absorb material and excel in a subject. They will make sure to find the answers to questions they have.

Common-sense learners focus on the "how." They want to reveal the connections to their life and why something matters to them. They are practical people who are willing to try different things. Coaching or tutoring is important for them.

Dynamic learners concentrate on the "what if..." question. They challenge what is told to them. They push the boundaries to uncover the full extent of what they can learn. Exploring new ideas and new methods are very important for this group of learners.

These four learning styles types may be a bit abstract at this point, and they are meant to be. The "4MAT" learning styles don't really prescribe ways that you should learn, as much as identify your tendencies. Also, if you get too specific and label yourself, you might miss out on other ways to learn which may be suitable for your needs too.

Now let's move on to another type of learning styles -- sensory learning styles -- because taking advantage of this will be the crux of how you will learn Spanish. Everyone learns by using their senses, especially their eyes, ears, and by touching. Our senses provide us with the important detailed information we need to process and learn from an experience. For example, touching a hot stove sends our brain signals and we learn never to do that again – and that's one area where pretty much everyone clearly takes advantage of their tactile sense best. Next, you will consider how you receive information and the best way you learn by using your senses. As you read, think about what methods you gravitate to when learning something new.

Visual Learners: These learners receive information by watching and seeing how things are done. Reading, viewing charts, graphs, tables and connecting images with what they mean are ways of processing that visual learners can take full advantage of. Picture-themed books are great ways to learn as well as watching videos.

Auditory Learners: This learning style focuses on what is heard, so listening plays an extremely important role for auditory learners. These learners do best by hearing things explained to them, or listening to various pronunciations and accents, or hearing lessons set to music. If you're an auditory learner, listening to the radio, podcasts, audio discs, and discussions of ideas and concepts are great ways to engage you. Of course, another thing that you hear is your own speech -- so practicing your Spanish out loud by having conversations, or repeating what you hear, is another method that is extremely well-suited to auditory learners. (Of course, it's important for everyone who wants to learn Spanish, even if "auditory" isn't your number one learning style.) Discover methods to activate your sense of hearing to maximize learning Spanish.

Kinesthetic Learners: The final important sense is touch or feeling. These learners advance faster by doing things themselves. Go out and try using your Spanish in active ways. Explain how to do things to others in a group discussion while you show them. Take a trip to a Spanish-speaking country. Take part in a Spanish club. Be a real "go-getter"!

Perhaps you have some idea what learning style category you fit into. Maybe you need some additional help determining your style. You can take an "inventory test" about learning styles based on Dr. James Thompson's work. (The link is in the "Resources" section at the end of the book.) Don't dwell too much on each question, and the whole test should only take you a few minutes to complete. Once you submit your answers, you will find which is your dominant learning style. Use this knowledge to consider which of the methods that we've discussed are most appropriate and will work best for you. Spend more time focusing on ways to learn Spanish that complement your learning style. This will help you show results in your language ability.

To check and make sure your assessment is correct, you should take another learning style inventory test – a re-test. You can do an Internet search using the keywords "learning style inventory" or "learning style assessment" to find more free tests. Another good site is LDPride.net. They have a fast, simple test where you select the answer that best fits you. In a matter of seconds, you will find out your learning style. Compare it with your first results. (The link to that test is also in the "Resources" section.)

If there's a discrepancy, don't worry. Learning styles are not "exclusive" -- that is, you don't just have one. You may have one or two that are stronger for you than the others, but most people learn in many different ways. It's just that you have strengths in certain areas that you should take advantage of, if you can. Whatever your results indicate, cater your Spanish learning toward the learning style or styles that best suit you. Don't ignore the other methods of learning because they focus on additional important aspects to the learning process. What I am saying is that you should use your main learning style methods heavily while using other learning methods to complement them. Let educators, instructors and tutors know what your learning style is so they may alter their teaching to address the way you learn best. If you can do that, you will find your learning experiences more enjoyable and productive.

It is my sincere hope that you have found some great ideas to master or improve your Spanish. I know you have the capability and determination to learn this beautiful language. After all, you have read this book. Now go out and make beautiful Spanish. *¡Buena suerte!*

RESOURCES

Here's a collection of wonderful resources to get you started on your path to Spanish fluency. Please note that these resources may not always be available, as products and websites change. These resources may also go through significant changes at any time since I've evaluated them for this book; however, use them as a starting point. Once you get used to knowing the kind of thing you're looking for, you can locate some up-to-date and useful resources for yourself. You may find many hidden treasures as you explore these resources, and as you search the web for more.

Learning Style Inventories

Dr. James Thompson,
http://people.usd.edu/~bwjames/tut/learning-style/stylest.html

LDPride.net, http://www.ldpride.net/learning-style-test.html

Books

Cambridge Word Selector, Cambridge University Press, ISBN: 0-521-42582-4

Easy Spanish Reader: A Three-Part Text for Beginning Students by William T. Tardy, National Textbook Company, ISBN: 0-8442-7051-2

The Firefly Spanish/English Visual Dictionary, Firefly Books, ISBN-13: 978-1-55407-717-5, ISBN-10: 1-55407-717-6

The New World Spanish/English, English/Spanish Dictionary, Salvatore Ramondino (editor), New American Library, ISBN-13: 978-0451181688, ISBN-10: 0451181689

The Oxford-Duden Pictorial Spanish and English Dictionary, Oxford University Press, ISBN: 0-19-864515-5

The Red-Hot Book of Spanish Slang: 5,000 Expressions to Spice Up Your Spanish by Mary McVey-Gill and Brenda Wegmann, McGraw-Hill, ISBN: 0-07-143301-5

Spanish Idioms by Eugene Savaiano, Ph.D. and Lynn W. Winget, Ph.D., Barron's Educational Series, Inc., ISBN: 0-8120-4637-4

The University of Chicago Spanish Dictionary, University of Chicago Press, ISBN-13: 978-0226666891, ISBN-10: 0226666891

Websites

Social Sites

Meetup.com, http://www.meetup.com/

My Language Exchange,
http://www.mylanguageexchange.com/

Live Mocha (language learning communities),
http://www.livemocha.com/

Spanish Search Engine

Terra-Lycos, http://www.terra.es/

Spanish Google, https://www.google.com/webhp?hl=es

Videos and More!

Barbara Kuczun Nelson's Spanish Language & Culture,
http://www.colby.edu/~bknelson/SLC/index.php

British Broadcasting Channel (BBC) Spanish,
http://www.bbc.co.uk/languages/spanish/

CNN in Spanish, http://cnnespanol.cnn.com/

LoMásTv (Spanish Immersion TV), http://lomastv.com/

Memoria de España (All-in-Spanish history of Spain),
http://www.rtve.es/alacarta/videos/memoria-de-espana/

Spanish Language TV Broadcasts, http://broadcast-live.com/television/spanish.html

Super Spanish Websites,
http://www.uni.edu/becker/Spanish3.html

Galavisión (a Spanish broadcasting station),
http://tv.univision.com/galavision/

Telemundo (a Spanish broadcasting station), http://msnlatino.telemundo.com/

Univisión (a Spanish news broadcasting station), http://noticias.univision.com/

Language Schools

Espanol Language School Directory, http://www.espanol.com/

Grammar and Fun

Notes in Spanish, http://www.notesinspanish.com/

Spanish Grammar Lessons, http://spanishgrammarlessons.com/

Software Programs

Byki Language-Learning Software (free Spanish flashcard program), http://www.byki.com/

BuenSoft Spanish, http://www.buensoft.com/english/download.htm

CNET Download, http://download.cnet.com/

Rosetta Stone: Spanish (all levels), http://www.rosettastone.com/

Transparent Language, http://transparent.com/

Apps

Spanish Flashcards by Bradley G. Hohn

Titulares by digital NOMAD

TuneIn Radio, http://tunein.com/

World Newspapers by Abhishek Kumar

ABOUT THE AUTHOR

Keith Walters has dedicated his life to helping others learn Spanish. Having studied the language through various methods and in native Spanish-speaking countries, his knowledge of what does and does not work is an excellent asset as you begin your language-learning journey. He offers private and small group Spanish lessons to individuals as well as businesses. He resides in Phoenix, Arizona, but can provide his language learning services throughout the world either using technology or by personal visitations. Please contact True Blue Dolphin Publishing to reach the author if you are interested in obtaining his services.

www.ingramcontent.com/pod-product-compliance
Lightning Source LLC
Chambersburg PA
CBHW071456070426
42452CB00040B/1538